IMAGES
of Wales

THE WELCH REGIMENT
(41ST AND 69TH FOOT)
1881-1969

A Guard of Honour of the 1st Battalion, The Welsh Regiment, at Pietermaritzburg, Natal, South Africa, 1883. Only the regimental helmet plate centre is worn on the white tropical helmet worn by the other ranks of the Battalion.

IMAGES
of Wales

THE WELCH REGIMENT
(41ST AND 69TH FOOT)
1881-1969

Compiled by
Bryn Owen FMA
for The Welch Regiment Museum

TEMPUS

First published 1999
Copyright © The Trustees, The Welch Regiment Museum, 1999

Tempus Publishing Limited
The Mill, Brimscombe Port,
Stroud, Gloucestershire, GL5 2QG

ISBN 0 7524 1679 0

Typesetting and origination by
Tempus Publishing Limited
Printed in Great Britain by
Midway Clark Printing, Wiltshire

Mounted Infantry of the 1st Battalion, The Welch Regiment, at Natal, South Africa, 1883. They wear the blue Glengarry Cap and on it is the regimental helmet plate centre with Victorian Crown above.

Contents

The Depot of The Welsh Regiment, Maindy Barracks, Cardiff, in 1881. Construction was completed in 1877 and this allowed occupation by the Sub District Brigade Depot staff and the permanent staff of the Royal Glamorgan Militia. Progressively between 1878 and 1881, the combined Depot staffs of the 41st (The Welch) Regiment and the 69th (South Lincolnshire) Regiment moved in from Fort Hubberstone, Pembrokeshire, and were firmly established there by July 1881. Thereafter and through to 1960 all recruits joining the Regiment underwent their preliminary training at this regimental centre.

Introduction

The Welch Regiment had its origins in two regiments, the 41st and 69th Regiments of Foot, the first of which has long standing links with the Royal Hospital, Chelsea – a link perpetuated to this day by the Royal Regiment of Wales.

The 41st was raised in March 1719 as a regiment of Invalids, namely Out-Pensioners of the Royal Hospital – men who, due to age and the wounds of previous wars, were considered to be unfit for active service, but were deemed to be perfectly suitable for garrison duties at home. Known as Lieutenant Colonel Fielding's Regiment of Foot (or The Invalids), the Regiment, between 1719 and 1787, carried out garrison duties in Portsmouth, Plymouth and the Channel Islands. However, the Regiment must not be confused with the twenty Independent Companies of Invalids who were active in the home garrisons during the same period.

In 1757 a second battalion was raised for the 24th Foot, and placed at the disposal of the Admiralty for service as marines with the fleet. In 1758 this Battalion was redesignated as the 69th Foot and, in 1782, linked to South Lincolnshire for recruiting purposes.

In 1787 the Invalid character of the 41st was abandoned and the Regiment re-formed as a marching regiment of the line fit for worldwide service. Between that date and 1881 the two Regiments pursued roles independent of one another, but drew closer when a common depot was established at Fort Hubberstone, Pembrokeshire, in 1871. Both campaigned and saw service in many parts of the world – achieving magnificent records of service – ultimately to be linked under the title 'The Welsh'.

The 41st saw service in the West Indies in the last decade of the eighteenth century and in 1798 was posted to Canada. There, its services in the Anglo/American War of 1812-14 ensured that Canada remained part of the British Empire, thus setting the foundations for the independent nation it is today. The Regiment also saw service in the Burma War of 1824-6. In 1831, while on service in India, it was territorialized for recruiting purposes as the 41st or The Welch Regiment of Infantry and thus became the indigenous infantry of South Wales. It served with distinction in the 1st Afghan War of 1842 and between 1854 and 1856 in the Crimea. In 1881, on being united with the 69th (South Lincolnshire) Regiment, it was redesignated as the 1st Battalion of The Welsh Regiment, a description which remained unchanged until 1920, when permission was given to revert to the original title 'The Welch'. This restored the original Old English spelling to the regimental title authorized by the King on its territorialization as the 41st (The Welch) Regiment of Infantry in 1831. The change brought to a close a long-standing dispute between the Regiment and the War Office regarding the correct historical title.

The 69th Foot also saw service in the West Indies in the 1790s and continued to provide detachments for service as marines with the fleet for almost forty years. That service saw the Regiment or detachments take part in some epic sea battles – The Saints (1782), the Glorious 1st (June 1794) and the Battle of St Vincent (1797). By this service it gained the unique distinction of being the only regiment in the British Army to gain two major naval battle honours, namely a Naval Crown superscribed '12th April, 1782' for the Saints and the scroll 'St Vincent 1797' for its part in that battle. Those honours were inherited first by The Welch Regiment and, in 1969, by the Royal Regiment of Wales. In addition to this service at sea, the 69th saw service at later dates worldwide. It was present at the Conquest of Java in 1811 and in action against Fenian insurgents in Canada in 1870. A second battalion, raised in 1803 and disbanded in 1816, brought the battle honour 'Waterloo' to its Colour. In 1881, on being united with the 41st, the 69th Foot became the 2nd Battalion, The Welsh Regiment, and soon became very Welsh in character.

Also included within the regimental fold in 1881 was the 3rd (Militia) Battalion, late Royal Glamorgan Militia and also four battalions of Rifle Volunteers which, in 1887, were designated as Volunteer Battalions of the Regiment. These units, in 1908, provided the nucleus for the formation of the 4th, 5th, 6th and 7th Battalions of the Regiment's Territorial Force and, in 1920, for the 4th, 5th and 6th Territorial Army Battalions of the Regiment.

After 1881 the two Regular Battalions of the Regiment saw service in many parts of the Empire including the North West Frontier of India. The First World War saw the Regiment expand to include thirty-five battalions, and was a period which, due to the nature of the fighting and heavy casualties, was destined to become one of the most traumatic, yet glorious, chapters in the regimental history. During the Second World War its combat battalions fought gallantly in Crete, North Africa, Sicily, Italy, North West Europe and Burma, adding significantly to an already long list of regimental battle honours. In 1948 the 2nd Battalion was sadly disbanded thus closing a distinguished record of service.

Between 1945 and 1969 the cold war confrontation and a withdrawal from Empire saw the surviving 1st Battalion serve in the Korean War, Germany, Cyprus, Libya and the Far East. In 1969 the Regiment celebrated its 250th Anniversary and then closed a magnificent record of service as 'The Welch' when, in June of the same year, at a ceremony held in the grounds of Cardiff Castle, it was amalgamated with the 1st Battalion, South Wales Borderers, to form the 1st Battalion, Royal Regiment of Wales (24th/41st Foot).

Recruits to the new Regiment, like those of its predecessor, come predominantly from South Wales, and the Regiment continues to maintain two museums; that of the 24th Foot (South Wales Borderers) and Monmouthshire Regiment at Brecon and The Welch in Cardiff Castle.

The photographs which form the content of this book are mainly taken from an extensive archive held in The Welch Regiment Museum (RRW) in Cardiff Castle, and I would like to extend my thanks to the Trustees. The selection is confined to the period 1881-1969, and it is hoped that the images will be of interest to those who are, or may become, involved in the history and services of an outstanding corps. There can be but few families with roots in South Wales who have not had links with this distinguished regimental family.

Bryn Owen FMA
Cardiff Castle, 1998

One
881-1914

Lieutenant Colonel A.B. Tulloch and some officers of the 1st Battalion, The Welsh Regiment, at Pietermaritzburg, Natal, South Africa, c. 1885. A wide variety of civil and military dress is worn by the officers.

Second Lt Charles M. Hastings of the 3rd (Militia) Battalion, *c.* 1885. He wears a dark blue patrol jacket and a Glengarry cap with a large plated cap badge consisting of the plumes, coronet and motto of the Prince of Wales.

Major George Frederick Heyworth, 3rd Militia Battalion and late 5th Dragoon Guards, in full dress uniform, *c.* 1885.

The 1st Battalion, The Welsh Regiment, marching through the Muski, Cairo, 1888. This photograph was taken from a painting held by the 2nd Battalion RRW.

The Goat Mascot, Taffy 1, belonging to the 2nd Battalion, The Welsh, *c.* 1888.

Warrant Officers and Sergeants of the 1st Battalion in Egypt, 1888. Seated at the front, next to the Mounted Infantry Company Sergeant (second left, front row, wearing leggings), is the Drum Major and Private Gwilym Jenkins, the Battalion Goat Mascot.

The 1st Battalion, Malta, 1890. The Sergeant Major is sat in the centre with the Colour Sergeants and Private Gwilym Jenkins.

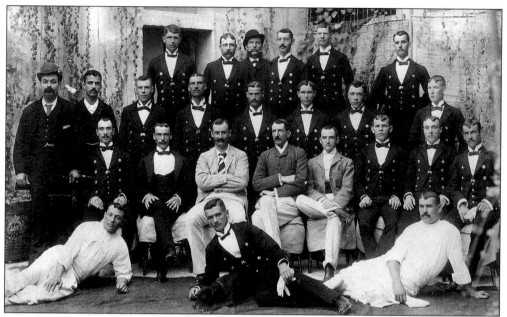

Some Officers and Officers' Mess Staff of the 1st Battalion, Malta, 1892. Left to right, back row: Pte 05 Hodges, Pte 01 Cook, -?-, -?-, -?-, Pte 62 Cheeseman. Second row from the back: -?-, -?-, Pte 19 Nicholls, Pte 38 Meadows, Pte Jones, -?-, Pte Law, Pte Renn. Third row: Pte Hall, Sgt 83 Curnow, Lt N.T. Borton, Captain L.H. Hawkes, Lt W. Scott, Cpl 05 Downs, Pte Joy, Pte 30 Jones. Front row: Pte West, Pte Prothero, Pte Mathews.

'H' Company, 2nd Battalion, The Welsh Regiment, at Aldershot in 1892. In September of that year the Battalion embarked for India and *en route* were reunited briefly with the 1st Battalion in Malta – an occasion of much cordiality.

The 2nd Battalion on the march during manoeuvres near Secunderabad, Hyderabad, India, in 1892.

The 2nd Battalion on manoeuvres near Secunderabad, Hyderabad, India, in 1892. As can be seen here, slit trenches were not a Second World War innovation.

The 1st Battalion, The Welsh Regiment, firing a *Feu de Joie* at Floriana Casemates, Malta, 24 May 1893. They are overlooking the Grand Harbour.

1st Battalion shooting team in Malta, 1893. Left to right, back row: Cpl Turner, Cpl 23 Davies, Pte 81 Andrews, Sgt 83 Jenkins, Pte 43 Johns, Pte 29 Haskins, L. Cpl Hancock, -?-, Pte Poole. Front row: Pte Mercer, Dmr Middleton, Dmr Jeninson, Dmr Sullivan, Dmr Cole, Dmr 54 Rees, Dmr Niblett, Dmr 78 Lucas. Seated at the front: Sgt 01 Acraman. Several of the men are wearing the ribbons of the Egypt Medal 1882-9 and the Khedives Bronze Star.

1st Battalion Guard Mounting Ceremony, Governor's Palace, Valetta, Malta, in 1893.

Private Gwilym Jenkins – the Goat Mascot of the 1st Battalion. Gwilym was fond of beer and tobacco and, for this reason, he aroused the wrath of non-conformist chapel ministers in South Wales on his return to the principality with the Battalion in 1893, and was described by them as displaying two of the worst characteristics of the British soldier. He was, however, extremely popular with the Welsh population and aroused much press interest.

A poster announcing the review of the 1st Battalion, the 3rd Battalion and the South Wales Volunteer Infantry Brigade at Margam Park, 8 August 1895.

GRAND REVIEW
OF THE
Gallant 41st,
Militia and Volunteers
Now stationed at Porthcawl, and numbering over **6000**, at
MARGAM PARK,
On Thursday Next, Aug. 8th, *1895*
Between 11 a.m. & 3 p.m.,
(By kind permission of MISS TALBOT.)

ADMISSION - - FREE.

☞ DEWCH YN LLUOEDD I'W CROESAWU.

REFRESHMENTS
Supplied to the public by
D. JONES,
PURVEYOR,
ASSEMBLY . ROOMS, ABERAVON.

T. Davies, Printer, Water-st., Aberavon.

The shooting team of the 3rd Glamorgan Rifle Volunteer Corps (Swansea), who were winners South Wales Volunteer Infantry Brigade Cup in 1895. Left to right. back row: Col. Sgt Beck, Pte Bob Rees, Sgt Tucker Williams, Col. Sgt F.N. Raggett, -?-, Pte D.J. Morris. Front row: Sgt Newman, Staff Sgt Major Mason, Captain M.J. Langdon, Sgt G.S. Harries.

1st Battalion Drum Major McKelvey and the Battalion Goat Mascot in Plymouth, 1896.

Quarter Guard of the 1st Battalion at the main gate of the Plymouth Citadel, 1896. The 41st or 'Invalids' had also garrisoned the Citadel in the early years of the eighteenth century.

Non-Commissioned Officers of the Cardiff Detachment, 3rd Volunteer Battalion, The Welsh Regiment, posing during Queen Victoria's Diamond Jubilee celebrations in 1897.

1st Battalion Church Parade, Aldershot, 1897.

The 2nd Battalion in Square at Bellary, Madras, India, in 1898.

The Band of the 2nd Battalion at Bellary, Madras, India, in 1898. The plumes, coronet and motto of the Prince of Wales, on a red cloth backing, are worn as the helmet plate.

The interior of a rather sparsely furnished but airy barrack room at Satara, Bombay, India, in 1899.

Lieutenant W.E.L. Stuart (mounted, right) and the smartly turned out Maxim Gun Detachment of the 1st Battalion at Aldershot in 1899.

The 1st Battalion at Aldershot, prior to their departure for South Africa and the Boer War in November 1899.

Lt Colonel R.J.F. Banfield (fourth from the right) and officers of the 1st Battalion, prior to embarking for South Africa in 1899. The Regimental Goat Mascot, as was customary, accompanied the Battalion to war.

The 1st Battalion disembark by tug boat from the SS *Kildonnan Castle* at Port Elizabeth, Cape Colony, on 26 November 1899. In February 1900 they joined Lord Roberts' army and thereafter saw two years of hard campaigning.

The Guard Room at the Camp of the 1st Battalion, Port Elizabeth, Cape Colony, South Africa, December 1899. There, the Battalion was acclimatized prior to moving up to the front.

A poster calling for volunteers to form the 1st Volunteer Active Service Company of The Welsh Regiment. This was one of three which saw active service with the 1st Battalion in South Africa between 1900 and 1903. The officers and men were drawn from the four South Wales Volunteer Battalions of the Regiment.

1st Battalion, The Welsh Regiment, entering Bloemfontein, 29 May 1900.

Private 769 (later RSM) J. Stuart of the Welsh Regiment Company, 6th Mounted Infantry, in South Africa in 1902. The vacancy caused by the absence of this company from the Regiment was filled in succession by the three Volunteer Active Service Companies of the Regiment.

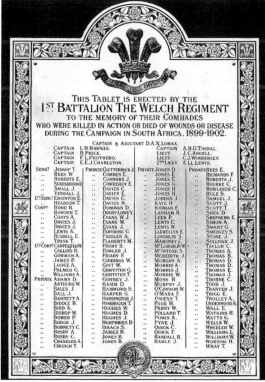

THIS TABLET IS ERECTED BY THE
1ST BATTALION THE WELCH REGIMENT
TO THE MEMORY OF THEIR COMRADES
WHO WERE KILLED IN ACTION OR DIED OF WOUNDS OR DISEASE
DURING THE CAMPAIGN IN SOUTH AFRICA, 1899-1902.

CAPTAIN & ADJUTANT D.A.N.LOMAX.

CAPTAIN	L.H.HAWKES.		CAPTAIN	A.H.U.TINDAL.
CAPTAIN	R.PRICE.		LIEUT.	J.C.ANGELL.
CAPTAIN	F.L.PROTHERO.		LIEUT.	C.J.WIMBERLEY.
CAPTAIN	E.E.J.CHARLETON.		2ND LIEUT.	E.LL.LEWIS.

SERGT	JESSOP T.	PRIVATE	CLUTTERBUCK J.	PRIVATE	JONES D.	PRIVATE	REES E.
,,	REES W.	,,	COMBES E.	,,	JONES E.	,,	RICHARDS F.
,,	ROBERTS E.	,,	CONNORS J.	,,	JONES E.	,,	ROBERTS J.
,,	SANDSBROOK D.	,,	COWDEROY E.	,,	JONES G.	,,	ROURKE C.
,,	SMALL J.	,,	DAVIES C.	,,	JONES H.	,,	ROWLANDS C.
,,	YENDALL J.	,,	DAVIES E.	,,	JONES H.	,,	RULE S.
L.CE SERGT	EDGINTON E.	,,	DAVIES C.	,,	JORDAN J.	,,	SAMUEL J.
,,	HEADDON T.	,,	DAVIES H.	,,	KAYE H.	,,	SCOTT J.
CORPL	BOND H.	,,	DONOVAN D.	,,	KIDMAN F.	,,	SCOTT T.
,,	BOWDEN T.	,,	DRURY-LOWE V.	,,	LANHAM R.	,,	SHEA D.
,,	COATS A.	,,	EVANS W.J.	,,	LEEK P.	,,	SHEPHERD E.
,,	DAVIES J.	,,	EVANS W.	,,	LEWIS C.	,,	SIMON A.
,,	DAVIES J.	,,	EVANS J.	,,	LEWIS W.	,,	SMART G.
,,	LEWIS A.	,,	FARTHING G.	,,	LLEWELLYN E.	,,	SMEDLEY S.
,,	RUSSELL E.	,,	FIDDLER A.	,,	LOUGHLIN S.	,,	STONE J.
,,	TRASK T.	,,	FLAHERTY M.	,,	MAHONEY C.	,,	SULLIVAN J.
L.CE CORPL	CARPENTER W.	,,	FOURY S.	,,	McLOUGHLIN W.	,,	TAYLOR C.
,,	COLLINS R.	,,	FOWLER J.	,,	McINTOSH S.	,,	THOMAS A.
,,	GOWMAN A.	,,	FRIARY F.	,,	MEREDITH J.	,,	THOMAS B.
,,	JAMES P.	,,	GIDDINGS W.	,,	MORGAN A.	,,	THOMAS D.
,,	LODGE A.	,,	GIST W.	,,	MORRIS A.	,,	THOMAS D.
,,	PALMER G.	,,	GRIFFITHS G.	,,	MORRIS J.	,,	THOMAS E.
,,	WILLIAMS A.	,,	GRIFFITHS T.	,,	MORRIS W.	,,	THOMAS J.
PRIVATE	ADAMS D.	,,	GURNEY J.	,,	MOSS H.	,,	THORNE C.
,,	ARTHURS W.	,,	HAMM D.	,,	MURPHY J.	,,	TODD J.
,,	BALES J.	,,	HAMMOND S.	,,	O'CONNOR W.	,,	TRANTER J.
,,	BALL J.	,,	HARPER G.	,,	O'MARA F.	,,	TRIGG E.
,,	BARNETT A.	,,	HARRINGTON J.	,,	OWENS T.	,,	TROLLEY A.
,,	BIDDLE H.	,,	HORRIGAN T.	,,	PAGE W.	,,	UNDERWOOD A.
,,	BIRD A.	,,	HUGHES W.	,,	PARRY W.	,,	WALL E.
,,	BISHOP W.	,,	HUGHES D.	,,	POLLARD T.	,,	WATKINS R.
,,	BOWEN P.	,,	HUGHES J.	,,	POWIS A.	,,	WATTS G.
,,	BUDGE J.	,,	HUMPHRIES D.	,,	PYNE J.	,,	WELLS W.
,,	BURNETT C.	,,	ISAACS S.	,,	QUICK C.	,,	WHEELER W.
,,	BUSBY A.	,,	JAMES H.	,,	QUICK F.	,,	WILLIAMS L.
,,	BUSBY C.	,,	JONES B.	,,	RANDALL R.	,,	WILLIAMS W.
,,	CHANDLER A.	,,	JONES B.	,,	RAWLE J.	,,	WORSOM H.
,,	CHURCH T.					,,	WRAY T.

The 1st Battalion Boer War Memorial Plaque at Llandaff Cathedral, Cardiff.

Lieutenant Colonel Alfred Thrale Perkins. He commanded the 3rd (Militia) Battalion in South Africa (1900–02) and received the Distinguished Service Order for his services.

The return of the 3rd (Militia) Battalion from South Africa in 1901. The Battalion is shown marching along the spectator-packed Crwys Road in Cardiff *en route* to the Regimental Depot.

A smart Sergeant of the 1st Volunteer Active Service Company, The Welsh Regiment. This picture was taken at Maindy Barracks, Cardiff, prior to departure for one year of active service in February 1900.

Boers attacking a derailed train near Godwan on 20 May 1902. The attackers were driven off with the assistance of a patrol of the 2nd Volunteer Active Service Company, The Welsh Regiment.

Officers of the 3rd Glamorgan Rifle Volunteer Corps in camp at Salisbury Plain in the Summer of 1902. Left to right, back row: Captain L. Thomas, Captain T. Mitchell, Captain Blenkinsop, Surgeon Major Jones, Revd W Morgan, Lt Coward, Lt Morgan. Seated: Major Thomas, Lt Colonel W.D. Rees, Colonel J.C. Richardson, Capt and Adjt H. Schofield, Major M.J. Langdon, Major D. Lewis. At the front: an unknown cyclist officer and Cyclist Lt Perkins.

A drummer from the 1st Battalion, c. 1902. His bugle cords are in the regimental colours: white, red and green.

Sergeant 7482 E. Lidyard of Aberdare
and the 3rd Volunteer Battalion, The
Welsh Regiment. He served as a
Private with the 2nd Volunteer Active
Service Company, The Welsh
Regiment, in South Africa.

A winter scene, Quetta, India, 1903. Men of the 2nd Battalion can be seen relaxing after a
snowball battle.

The Tirah Goat. 1905
2nd Battalion, The Welch Regt

The Drum Major and Goat Mascot of the 2nd Battalion, India, 1905. The goat, of Afghan origins, was presented to the Battalion by the Amir of Tirah following upon the death of the Battalion's Royal Goat Mascot.

The 2nd Battalion in India, 1905. The Tirah Goat was a magnificent beast who, when standing on his hind legs, was over 6ft in height.

Regimental Police of the 1st Battalion at Gravesend in 1905. They wear the unpopular Broderick cap which was introduced in 1902 and phased out in 1905.

A 2nd Battalion Guard of Honour for the visit of the HRH The Prince of Wales to Quetta, India, in 1906. In the background the snow-clad mountains of the Afghan frontier can be seen.

The visit of HRH The Prince and Princess of Wales to Quetta, Baluchistan, in 1906. With the officers of the 2nd Battalion are the following dignitaries, left to right: Mrs B.T. Ready, a lady-in-waiting, HRH The Prince of Wales, Mrs W.V. Dickinson, Mrs C.H. Young, HRH Princess Mary of Wales, Lady Smith-Dorrien, Mrs T.M. Sprent.

The bayonet team of the 2nd Battalion, at Quetta, Baluchistan, in 1906. Private 113 F. Ferrisey, second from the right, back row, was an expert in this particular sport.

Viscount Kitchener of Khartoum with officers of the 1st Battalion on the occasion of the presentation of new Colours to the Battalion at Alexandria, Egypt, on 13 December 1910. Left to right, back row: Lt Todd (RAMC), Captain Darrell (ADC), Lt Dickinson. Middle row: Lt Westby, Lt Montgomery, Captain Torkington, Lt Salmon, Lt (QM) Holt, Captain Pake, Major Hoggan, Lt Banfield, Lt Lloyd, Lt Penno, 2nd Lt Phillips. Front row: Captain Derry, Captain Broughton, Major General Sir J. Maxwell, Lt Colonel Schofield (CO), Viscount Kitchener, Major Prothero, Colonel Pinney, Major Ready.

The regimental barracks of 2nd Battalion, The Welsh, at Bloemfontain, South Africa, in 1907.

Officers and Non-Commissioned Officers of the 1st Battalion Mounted Infantry Detachment in Egypt, 1910.

The 2nd Battalion on Public Duties in London, August 1910. Here, the Buckingham Palace Guard are formed up at Wellington Barracks.

"C" Block Infantry Married Quarters

The 2nd Battalion's 'other ranks' married quarters at Llanyon Barracks, Pembroke Dock, 1910.

'Catch 'em Young' – Eleven-year-old bugler, Bertie Williams, 4th Battalion (TF) at Lamphey, Haverfordwest, Brigade Camp, 1910. Bertie was embodied with the Battalion in August 1914, but due to his age was discharged and sent home to his mother.

Officers of the 5th Battalion (TF) Brigade Camp, Lamphey, Haverfordwest, 1911. Left to right, back row: Capt. J.G. Jones, Capt. H.H.W. Southey, Capt. W. Dowdeswell, Capt. D. Harris, Lt H.V. Leigh, Lt T.R. Dowdeswell, Lt T.W.P. Evans. Middle row: Surgeon Capt. E.J.T. Cory, Lt A.O. Mander, Lt T.A. Evans, Lt D.P. Robathan, Chaplain E.T. Davies, Lt D. Morgan, Lt R.D. Williams, Capt. G.A. Evans. Front row: Capt. F.N. Gray, Major J.S. Davies, Lt Colonel M. Morgan VD, Colonel A.P. James VD, Major W.D. Phillips VD, Capt and Adjt M. Haggard, Major T. Tinnock.

The 2nd Battalion, The Welsh Regiment, leave Pembrokeshire for Liverpool on 17 August 1911.

Camel Mounted Signals Section, 1st Battalion, The Welsh Regiment, Egypt, 1911.

'Home from Home' – Private 639 P.
Williams, 1st Battalion, The Welsh
Regiment, in his corner of the Barrack
Room, Cairo, in 1911.

Sergeant Major May-Hill (centre) and the Colour Sergeants of the 1st Battalion, Egypt, 1912. Several are wearing the Queen's and King's South Africa Medal for Boer War Service.

A Sergeant from the 7th (Cyclist) Battalion, The Welsh Regiment (TF), c. 1912. The full dress uniform was rifle green with red facings; badges and buttons were black. Black polished leather equipment was also worn and the head-dress was the Rifles' busby.

'D' Company, 2nd Battalion, led by Captain W.A.G. Moore, marching through Eastleigh, Hants, *en route* to Aldershot for manoeuvres, 1913. Captain Moore was killed in action at Gheluveldt near Ypres, Belgium, on October 1914.

The 1st Battalion silver centrepiece, commissioned in the 1890s. It depicts the Saving of the Colours at the Battle of Inkerman, The Crimea, 5 November 1854.

Men of the 8th (Service) Battalion under training in the grounds of Cardiff Castle, late August 1914. The Service Battalion men were Kitchener Volunteers who had enlisted for three years, or the duration of the war. The Battalion later saw service in Gallipoli and in the Middle East. The Castle has strong regimental links and was, between 1881 and 1969, the venue for many regimental functions and much ceremonial activity.

Two

1914-1918

For gootness sake go back! Here kom
der WELCH.

This type of cartoon postcard, with its mixture of humour and propaganda, was mass
produced and very popular.

Left to right: Captain C. Perry, Lt F.S. Hinton and Lt Carl Langer of the 6th Battalion (TF) at King's Dock, Swansea, August 1914. They wear, above the right breast pocket, the Imperial Service badge which indicates that they had volunteered for active service abroad.

Church Parade, 6th Battalion (TF), at Swansea shortly after embodiment for war service in August 1914. The Battalion was one of the first Territorial Force Battalions to embark for France in October 1914.

Recruits to the 11th (Service) Battalion 'Cardiff Pals' still in civilian dress, march down Crwys Road, Cardiff, to entrain for Lewes, Sussex, in September 1914. The Battalion later saw service in France and Macedonia.

Battle of the Aisne, September 1914. Captain Mark Haggard, 2nd Battalion, was mortally wounded during an attack on Chivy Ridge, but is represented here urging his men on with the battle cry 'Stick it, The Welch'. He was carried back to a first aid post under heavy fire by Lance Corporal William Fuller of Swansea who was later awarded the Victoria Cross for his valour.

Sergeant William Fuller VC from Swansea. He was the third regimental recipient of the Victoria Cross and the first of three members of the Regiment to receive the award during the First World War.

Recruits to the 13th (Service) Battalion (2nd Rhondda) on parade in Cardiff prior to their departure for North Wales and further training. The Battalion later saw service in France and Flanders with the 38th (Welsh) Division.

Men of the 3rd (Special Reserve) Battalion under training in Bute Park, Cardiff, October 1914. The Battalion provided a steady stream of reinforcement drafts for the 1st and 2nd Battalions of the Regiment throughout the war.

Major E.A. Pope leading a detachment of the 3rd (Special Reserve) Battalion out of Cardiff Castle on a recruiting march through the City in Autumn 1914. In 1916 the Battalion moved to Kinmel Park Camp, North Wales, then to Redcar, Yorkshire, in 1917 and in l918 to Chatham, Kent.

Recruiting in September 1914. Corporal Franklin, a well-known music hall comedian, can be seen recruiting in Cardiff for the 17th and 18th (Service) Battalions (1st and 2nd Glamorgan Bantam Battalions).

A draft of the 2/7th (Cyclist) Battalion (TF) at Victoria railway station, London, *en route* to join the 1/7th Battalion on the North East Coast defenses, November 1914.

Lieutenant Colonel T.O. Marden (right) and
the 1st Battalion on a route march near
Winchester, January 1915. Shortly thereafter
the Battalion embarked for France and
service on the Western Front.

8th (Service) Battalion Goat Major and
Goat Mascot, c. 1915.

Drums and Fifes, 9th (Service) Battalion, at Weston-Super-Mare in March 1915. The Battalion later saw service in France and Flanders.

Men of the 6th Battalion (TF), early in 1915. They wear sheepskin coats to protect them from the cold, although this was already a natural protection for their Goat Mascot.

Troops leave Cardiff for the Front in 1915. A curious boy watches as a lady hands out comforts.

Soldiers of the 16th (Service) Battalion (Cardiff City) with the Battalion Goat Mascot at Colwyn Bay, North Wales, in May 1915. They wear, as collar badges, the Arms of the City of Cardiff.

Officers of the 15th (Service) Battalion (Carmarthenshire) at Rhyl, North Wales, May 1915.
Left to right, back row (staggered): A. Lewis, T. Landman, F. Roberts, D.S. Davies, W. Reese,
? Hamilton-Lloyd, A.G. Corser, J. Skelding, T.L. Morgan, W.B. Protheroe, Douglas Jones,
R. Burgess. B.A. Lewis. Middle row: Captain H. Gardiner (QM), Lt W. Soden (RAMC), Lt J.
McDonald, Lt P.L. Humphreys, Lt A.E. Edwards, 2nd Lt G.A. Griffiths, Lt E. Walker, Lt H.C.
Lewis, 2nd Lt T.L. Stewart. Front row: Capt P. Anthony, Major J.H. Rees, Major W.S.R. Cox,
Lt Colonel M.J.G. Scobie (CO), Lt & Adjt A. Rhudderch, Major J.K. Williams, Captain A.P.
Sprague, Capt D. Powell. At the front: Goat Mascot, Goat Major.

Soldiers of the 16th Battalion at bayonet practice in Colwyn Bay, North Wales, around May 1915. The Battalion later saw service in France and Flanders.

Drums and Fifes of the 17th (Service) Battalion (1st Glamorgan Bantams), Rhos on Sea, North Wales, around May 1915. The Bantams were recruited from men who under normal circumstances could not meet the basic height requirement; their average height was 5ft 2 inches. This Battalion also later saw service in France and Flanders.

Private 514 W.J. Badcock, Goat Major, 18th (Service) Battalion (2nd Glamorgan Bantams), at Preece Heath Camp, Salop, in 1915. All thirty-five Battalions of The Welsh Regiment followed the regimental custom of having a Goat Mascot. The goat, a hardy beast with great stamina, is a very appropriate mascot as it is agile, aggressive and can live on next to nothing; qualities that are also required in the soldier.

Soldiers of 'B' Company, 2nd Battalion, outside billets at Neuve Chapelle in 1915. They were still muddied from a recent spell in the trenches.

The 4th Battalion (TF) marching through Biggleswade, Bedfordshire, in 1915. The Battalion later saw service with the 53rd (Welsh) Division in Gallipoli and the Middle East.

In a communication trench at Givenchy in 1915 are, left to right: Captain Aldworth, Lt Leycester, Lt Betts and Lt Jones, officers of the 2nd Battalion. The Battalion, which had arrived in France as part of the British Expeditionary Force (BEF) in August 1914, served throughout the war on the Western Front.

1st Battalion night action on the Frezenberg Ridge, 7 May 1915. The remnants of 'A' Company, led by 2nd Lt E.W. Bryant, are seen here holding off an enemy attack. Bryant was awarded the Military Cross for his gallantry, the first to be received by an officer of the Battalion. The battle of Frezenburg Ridge, south of Ypres was fought in May 1915. On the night of the 6-7 May, 'A' Company on the 1st Battalion, The Welsh Regiment, moved up to support the Northumberland Fusiliers then under heavy attack. 'A' Company trenches came under heavy enemy bombardment and the Company suffered heavy losses. Under 2nd Lt Bryan's cheerful and firm leadership the survivors of the Company held on until they were relieved the following day.

What do you think of the WELSH now, Bill ?

A cartoon, used as a morale booster for families and friends at home. The Welch in France and Flanders knew better however, the German Armies were no 'push over'.

Wounded soldiers arrive back at Cardiff central station in 1915.

Soldiers of the 2nd Battalion in France in April 1916. Censorship did not allow publication of their location at the time but records show that on that date the Battalion was in the Loos sector of the Western Front.

Soldiers of 1/6th Battalion (TF). The Battalion was at this time (around June 1916) in a rear training area preparing for future action on the Somme.

Soldiers of the 53rd (Welsh) Division (including 4th and 1/5th Welsh) advance in open order across the Salt Lake, Suvla Bay, Gallipoli, in August 1915. The Turks held the high ground ahead of them.

Captain E.E. O'Donnell of the 8th (Service) Battalion, The Welsh Regiment, at Anzac Cove, Gallipoli, in 1915. The 8th Battalion served as the Pioneer Battalion on the 13th Division. During the assault on a Turkish position at Chunuk Bair on 8 August 1915, the Battalion lost 6 officers and 303 other ranks.

Soldiers of the 11th (Service) Battalion 'Cardiff Pals' at Salonika in Greece in 1916.

Officers of the 10th (Service) Battalion (1st Rhondda) in Reserve Billets near Ypres, 1917. Standing: W. Reynolds. E.J. Griffiths Seated: ? James, ? Bucknell, Gwynne Lewis.

6th Battalion (TF): 'Hope springs eternal'.
This is Lance Corporal E. Jones and his
mates in billets in France, 1916.

Lance Corporal V. Williams (right) and
another of the 6th Battalion (TF), somewhere
in France, June 1916.

Men of the 1/5th Battalion visiting the Sphinx and Pyramids at Gizeh, Egypt, 1916.

2/4th (Reserve) Battalion Fort Scoveston, Pembrokeshire, in March 1917. This shows a kit inspection of a draft prior to embarkation to join 1/4th Welsh in Egypt.

Young soldiers group 12th (Reserve) Battalion at Kinmel Park Camp, North Wales, in 1917.

Lieutenant H. Morrey Salmon, Adjutant 16th (Cardiff City) Battalion, poses behind hessian screens at Ypres Salient, 1917. He was later to be awarded the Military Cross and Bar. During the Second World War he raised and commanded the first Squadron of the RAF Regiment.

Officers of 'D' Company, 16th (Cardiff City) Battalion, dine in a front line trench at Morteldje, Ypres Salient, in October 1916. Included, left to right, in the foreground are: Captain M.G. Bostock (standing), Lt J.C.Jones, Lt T.B.Jones.

A typical Bantam soldier: a Sergeant from the 17th Battalion (1st Glamorgan Bantams), c. 1917. As casualties mounted, the Bantam character of these battalions receded, as recruits of regulation height replaced them.

Captain J. Gwyther Jones, on the right, and officers of the 18th Welsh (2nd Glamorgan Bantams) in a trench near Boulon Wood, Cambrai. The officers of the Battalion did not conform with the Bantam height limits and invariably were much taller than their men.

Victory Parade, Alexandria, Egypt, 2 December 1918. The composite Battalion, 4th/5th Welsh (TF), lead the victorious column.

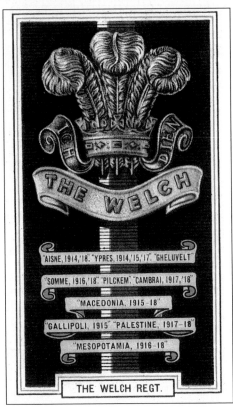

The 1920 pattern cap badge of The Welch Regiment. The cap badge worn prior to 1920 carried the scroll with the title 'THE WELSH'.

Three

1918-1939

The return of the 6th Battalion (TF), 1919. The Colours are from the Army of Occupation, Germany to Swansea. Left to right: Captain F.C. Palmer MC, CSM R. Davies, Captain H.M. Randell, Captain (QM) J.M.H. Russell.

The 2nd Battalion, winners Army Rugby Cup in the 1919/20 season. Left to right, back row: Captain C.E.N. Lomax, Captain B.M. Dunn, Major W.G. Hewett, Lt W.Y. Price, Lt R.M. Phillips, L. Cpl G. Williams. Middle row: Sgt D. Last, Dmr T. Payne, CSM C.W. Jones, Captain J.A. Daniel, Sgt D. Vaughan, Lt R.C. Linsey Brabazon, Lt E.S. Pincott. At the front: -?-, Taffy the Goat Mascot, Pte M. Morgan.

The 2nd Battalion on parade at Richmond Barracks, Dublin, July 1920. The period was one of Civil War in Southern Ireland and led up to the withdrawal of British troops and the establishment of the Irish Free State.

A change over at Richmond Barracks, Dublin, with Irish Free State government troops marching in and the 2nd Battalion, The Welch Regiment, marching out to embark for England. The old English format 'Welch' was authorized for use by the Regiment in 1920, so ending a dispute between the War Office and the Regiment which had lasted for almost ninety years.

1st Battalion Lines, Razmak Camp, Waziristan, North West Frontier, India, in 1922. For active service against Mahsud tribesmen, the Battalion qualified for the India General Service Medal with clasp 'Waziristan 1921-24'.

A 1st Battalion patrol near Razmak, Waziristan, 1923. Mules were used to carry heavy equipment.

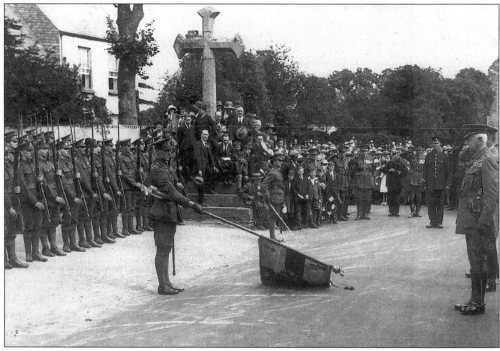

A Guard of Honour of the 6th Battalion (TA) in 1924. The Battalion was commanded by Major B. Williams, seen here at the unveiling of the Llandaff Cardiff War Memorial. The Regimental Colour is carried by Lt K.L.P. Ollson.

The 1st Battalion boxing team in India, *c.* 1924. Left to right, back row: -?-, Pte Evans, Pte 09 Jones, Pte Warwick. Front row: CSM Finnegan, Captain C.H. Kinnaird.

Warrant Officers and Sergeants at the Regimental Depot, Cardiff, in 1926. Left to right, back row: Sgt J. Robbins, Sgt F. Wilton, Sgt T.R. Morgan, Sgt H. Turner, L Sgt W. Farrow. Middle row: Sgt P. McCray, L Sgt F. Collyer, CQMS Daniel, Mr W. Chattin, L Sgt A. Cole, Sgt H. Shone, Sgt H. Tooze. Front row: Staff Sgt R. Beattie, QMS C. Williams MM, RSM G. Faulkener, Lt I.B.S. Lewin, Major F.H. Linton DSO, Major (QM) H.A. Weimers, RQMS A. Pettit DCM, CSM G.O. Burn MM, WO2 R. Shearer.

A Guard of Honour of the 6th Battalion (TA) at the opening ceremony of the National Museum of Wales by His Majesty King George V on 21 April 1927.

Signallers of the 4th Battalion, the Welch Regiment, at Porthcawl summer camp in 1927.

Officers of the 2nd Battalion at Tanglin Barracks, Singapore, on Christmas Day 1928. Left to right, back row: Goat Major and Regimental Goat Mascot, Dent, Whitty, Corbin, Griffiths, Welchman, August, Hirsch, Jones, Parry-Evans, -?-, Coleman. Front row: Morgan, Quinn, Cripps, Gransmore, Melville, Whitty, Lomax, McGroarty, Duncan.

An inspection of the 4th Battalion (TA) by the Colonel of the Regiment at Brigade Camp, Holyhead, in the Summer of 1929.

A party for families in the The Warrant Officers' and Sergeants' Mess at Tanglin Barracks, Singapore, on Christmas Day 1930.

'Boy Soldier' Hill of the 2nd Battalion in his barrack room at Muree Hills, India, 1931.

The 2nd Battalion Colours, Regimental Silver and other trophies on display at Victoria Barracks, Rawalpindi, on St David's Day 1932.

The 2nd Battalion on the march near Mansehra in November 1932. The Battalion was accompanied by its mule baggage train and a mass of Indian domestic servants which took up about two miles of road.

The 1st Battalion Goat Major, Goat Mascot and Band and Drums at Aldershot in 1933.

Inspection of 160th Infantry Brigade, 53rd (Welsh) Division, on Tenby Sands in August 1933. Included are the 4th, 5th and 6th (TA) Battalions of The Welch Regiment.

The presentation of leeks to members of the Depot Party at Maindy Barracks, Cardiff, on St David's Day, 1 March, *c.* 1934. The day was always observed as a regimental holiday when all ranks, in keeping with regimental tradition, wore the leek in their caps (see p. 108).

The Band and Drums of the 1st Battalion, on a visit of their Majesties, the King and Queen, to Aldershot in April 1934.

The opening of the new Civic Centre in Swansea on 23 October 1934. HRH The Duke of Kent can be seen inspecting a Guard of Honour of the 6th Battalion (TA) which was commanded by Captain C.G. Kerswell.

An inspection of a Company of the 5th Battalion (TA) by the Mayor of Basingstoke in September 1935. The Company had marched from Bristol to Basingstoke to join the Battalion and units of the regular army on manoeuvres.

The road and railway through the Khyber Pass to Landi Kotal. The 2nd Battalion was stationed in this North West Frontier garrison from December 1934 to March 1936. It was dangerous country, inhabited by unpacified and warlike tribesmen.

Hard graft: men of the 2nd Battalion, The Welch Regiment, cutting out a road near Landi Kotal, Waziristan, North West Frontier, 1935.

The 2nd Battalion participated in the filming of the Gaumont British film *Soldiers Three* near Landi Kotal on the North West Frontier, India, in 1935.

Pacified Afridi Tribesmen pose during the filming of *Soldiers Three*, Landi Kotal, North Western Frontier, India, in 1935.

Landi Kotal Camp, Waziristan, North West Frontier, India, 1935. The camp was protected by outposts on the surrounding mountains and by perimeter stone walls and stone sangers (raised stone defensive positions).

The Wedding of Lieutenant C.C. Coleman of the 2nd Battalion at Landi Kotal, North Western Frontier, December 1935. Families did not accompany the Battalion in this garrison but an exception was made to allow this, the first garrison wedding, to take place. As a Lieutenant General, Coleman was later Colonel of The Welch Regiment.

Major General Sir T.O. Marden KCB, CB, CMG taking the salute at the Trooping of the Colours ceremony at Victoria Barracks, Belfast, on 3 July 1936. The inset shows the presentation of the Long Service and Good Conduct Medal to Sergeant A. Jacob.

The Drums of the 2nd Battalion, at Agra, India, in 1936. In the centre is Drum Major E. Cates flanked by the Commanding Officer Lt Colonel A.G. Lyttleton (left) and Captain J.R. Welchman (right).

1st Battalion rugby team, winners of the Army Rugby Cup, 1937. Left to right, inset: L. Cpl C. Hopkins, Pte P. Cowell, L. Cpl I. Owen. Back row: L. Cpl D. Carney, Pte J. Delaney, Pte B. Pass, Pte E. Edwards, Pte W.E. Buss, L. Cpl J.H. Driscoll, Pte H.R. Coleman. Middle row: Pte E.G. Pennell, Sgt C.R. Owen, Lt B.T.V. Cowe, Sgt H. Ibbottson, Sgt W. William. Seated at the front: Pte T. Jones, Pte W. Thomas.

A Guard of Honour from the 6th Battalion (TA) for the visit of HM King George V to Swansea on 14 July 1937. The Guard Commander (right) is Captain G. Kerswell.

A regimental recruiting poster, c. 1938.

Four
1939-1945

New intakes to the 4th Battalion (TA) in Haverfordwest, 1940. The Battalion later saw service in Northern Ireland, France and North West Europe (1944-5).

Glamorgan Company Women's Auxiliary Training Corps at Maindy Barracks, Cardiff, 1939. As in the First World War, the contribution made by women to the war effort was immense and essential.

A 1st Battalion choir at Mersah Matruh, Spring 1940. The choirmaster (centre) was Lt Martin Verity. The Battalion later served in Crete, Egypt and the Sudan, Libya, Sicily and Italy.

The 1st Battalion at Khartoum, Sudan, in Spring 1942. After suffering heavy casualties in Crete the Battalion was re-formed and posted to Khartoum with one detachment at Kufra Oasis. Here the Battalion is being inspected by General Alexander.

Corporal Tommy Bevan MM, of Swansea and the 1st Battalion, who was taken prisoner by the Germans in Crete in 1941. Tommy escaped from a POW Camp in Salonika and made his way across southern Greece to the Aegean coast. In a stolen boat he rowed, with others, across the Aegean sea to Turkey, and from there made his way back to Egypt to rejoin the Battalion. He was one of the war's great escapers and was awarded the Military Medal for his courage and determination.

Rugby football team, 70th Home Service/Reserve Battalion Whittlesford, Cambridgeshire, around the Winter of 1942/3. Seated in the centre is the Commanding Officer, Lt Colonel H.C.L. Davies. On his left is the Adjutant, Captain R.E. Dunn. On his right is Lt K. Bloomer, then Captain W.R. Davies and Captain J.A. Daley.

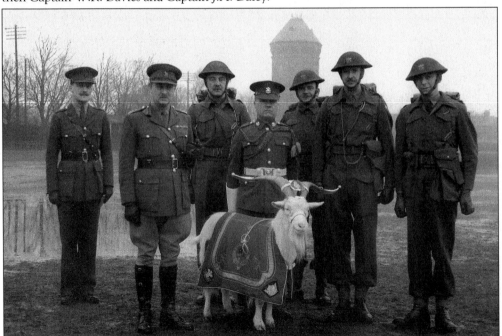

Goat Major and Goat Mascot of the 1st Battalion with officers and Sergeant Major Jelf (second from the left), 70th (HS) Battalion, at Hunstanton in January 1942.

Major General D.P. Dickinson CB, DSO, OBE, MC (centre), with Lt Colonel C.C. Coleman (left of Dickinson) and officers of the 4th Battalion (TA) at Faversham, Kent, in 1943.

A shooting team from the 21st Battalion, Glamorgan Home Guard, 1943. Left to right, back row: Pte Cattling, L. Cpl Davies, L. Cpl Hancock, Cpl Annan, Cpl Norris, Cpl Hinchley, Pte Beavis. Front row: Cpl Lloyd, Captain Sergeant, Lt Griffiths, Sgt Wilkins, Sgt Holley, Major Davies, Sgt Robinson. Many members of the Glamorgan Home Guard Battalions were regimental veterans of the First World War.

Lieutenant Tasker Watkins, 5th Battalion (TA), single-handedly destroying the second of two enemy positions which were holding up the movements of his Company near Bafour, Normandy, on 16 August 1944. Lieutenant Watkins was awarded the Victoria Cross for his leadership and valour.

Lt Colonel Morrison Jones of the 1/5th Battalion (TA) inspecting the Battalion at St Quentin, Belgium, 1944. Morriston Jones was killed in action when his jeep was blown up by a land mine during the advance into Germany in April 1945.

Men of the 1/5th Battalion undergo amphibious training in Holland, 1944. The Battalion, as part of the 53rd (Welsh)Division, fought its way through from Normandy to Hamburg during the North West Europe campaign of 1944-5.

Mortar Platoon of the 1/5th Battalion (TA) at Weert, Holland, November 1944. The Mortar Platoon were equipped with the 3 inch mortar which fired a 10 pound high explosive or smoke bomb. With an effective range of 1,600 yards, the weapon was a useful tool in supporting infantry attacks with accurate high explosive bombardment and providing protective smoke screen cover for the advancing troops.

'Char and Wads': men of 1/5th Battalion (TA) YMCA mobile canteen at Weert, Holland, November 1944. Manned by volunteers, these canteens did much to boost the morale of the troops.

A Cadre of the 1st Battalion at Porto Potenza, Italy, December 1944. Due to heavy casualties the Battalion was reduced to cadre strength in September 1944. Some two months later the Battalion was re-formed from drafts of Welshmen and others serving with the British Army in Italy. The Battalion continued to serve in Italy until 1947.

The Band of the 15th Home Service/Reserve Battalion at Stromness, Orkney Islands, 1944. The Battalion served in many parts of the United Kingdom and provided reinforcement drafts for the active service battalions of the Regiment overseas.

The field kitchen of the 1/5th Battalion (TA) at Rechswald Forest in February 1945. The 4th Battalion (TA) also took part in the battle.

'D' Company HQ, 1/5th Battalion (TA), at Reichswald Forest in February 1945. The fighting here was reminiscent of the wood battles of the Western Front, 1916-17.

Men of the 1/5th Battalion (TA) in a slit trench Reichswald Forest, February 1945.

'*En route* to Blighty': a battle casualty from the 1/5th Battalion (TA) Reichswald Forest battle in February 1944. Battalion casualties in this battle totalled 4 officers and 121 other ranks.

1/5th Battalion (TA) positioned in a ditch on the route to the Rhine Holland in 1945. Note the rough corrugated iron sheet shelters.

A Company from 1/5th Battalion (TA) on the march towards the Rhine in March 1945.

1/5th Battalion on the march along the Hamburg road in April 1945.

German prisoners of war employed as stretcher bearers by the 1st/5th Battalion, The Welch Regiment, on Hamburg Road in April 1945.

A soldier of the 2nd Battalion poses for a photograph during a rest period during the Burma Campaign, 1945. Steel helmets were discarded in favour of bush hats. He is carrying the No. 4 (.303 Cal) Rifle.

Signallers from the 2nd Battalion during the Burma campaign, 1945. The Battalion, which had been out east since 1927, did not return to the United Kingdom until 1947.

The Band and Drums of the 1/5th Battalion Army of Occupation in Dusseldorf, Germany, in 1945.

Sgt George Bower MM and Sgt Major Johnny Evans MM, both of the 1st/5th Battalion, The Welch Regiment. They were awarded the Military Medal for gallantry during the North West Europe campaign of 1944-5.

The Armistice Day Ceremony at the Cenotaph, Maindy Barracks, Cardiff, on 11 November 1945.

Five

1945-1969

The Colour Party of the 2nd Battalion. The Colour Officers are: Lt Hale (left) and Lt Stibbs (right) at Kalaw, Burma, 1946. The Colours were destroyed by fire on 27 December 1946 and were the last to be carried by the Battalion.

Warrant Officers and Sergeants of the 1st Battalion at Gradisca, near Trieste, Italy, Summer 1946. Left to right, back row: Sgt Silvester, CQMS Cummings, SSI Eastham, Sgt Wills, -?-, Sgt Pritchard, Sgt Scott, Sgt Whelan. Second row from the back: Sgt Higgon, Sgt Williams, Sgt Beban, Sgt Armstrong, -?-, Sgt Done, Sgt Garth, Sgt Dry, Sgt 05 Rees, Sgt Berry. Third row: Sgt 17 Williams, Sgt Richardson, Sgt Watts, CQMS Williams, Sgt Aston, -?-, Sgt Steer, Sgt Masters, -?-, Sgt Dykes, Sgt Whitley. Front row: CQMNS Perryman, CSM Lewis, CSM Austin, Captain J. F. Blanche, Lt Colonel D.L.C. Reynolds OBE, CSM Cannon, CSM Crawford, CSM Dearden, CQMS Hill.

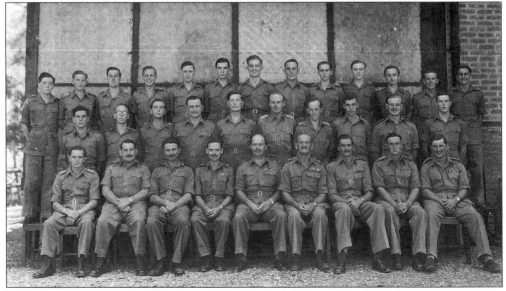

Lt Colonel B.T.V. Cowey DSO (front row, centre) and the officers of the 2nd Battalion in Burma in 1946.

CORPS OF DRUMS 4th BN·THE WELCH REGIMENT 1946

The Band and Drums and the Goat Mascot of the 4th Battalion (TA), the Army of Occupation at Dusseldorf, Germany, 1946.

4th Battalion (TA) on parade at Llanelly Barracks in Dusseldorf, Germany, in the Spring of 1946. The Battalion was, at this date, serving with the 49th (West Riding) Division.

The 4th Battalion (TA) at Llanelly Barracks, Dusseldorf, Germany, Spring 1946. The Battalion, as part of the British Army of Occupation in Germany, was heavily involved in supporting the restoration of German civil administration, policing and searching for war criminals and directing the repatriation of thousands of displaced European nationals.

The 2nd Battalion on parade at Kalaw, Burma, 1946.

The Band of the 1st Battalion at Udine Cavalry Barracks in Italy, Spring 1947.

A Guard of Honour from the 2nd Battalion on the visit of HRH Princess Elizabeth to Cardiff on 27 May 1947. The Goat Mascot of the 1st Battalion kneels before the future Queen.

The Guard of Honour from the
2nd Battalion at Cardiff Docks on
18 June 1947. This ceremony
marked the occasion of the return of
4,000 caskets containing the
remains of American Second World
War dead to the USA on the US
transport *Lawrence Victory*. The
Battalion was amalgamated with the
1st Battalion in 14 June 1948.

The presentation of the New
Colours to the 1st Battalion, Dering
Lines, Brecon, 17 September 1948.
Major General D.P. Dickinson CBE,
DSO, OBE, MC, Colonel of the
Regiment, acts on behalf of His
Majesty the King.

The 5th Battalion (TA) marching through Pontypridd, 11 November 1948.

The Colonel of the Regiment, Major General C.E.N. Lomax CB, CBE, DSO, MC (centre, front row), and the Commanding Officer, Lt Colonel H.H. Deane (to the left of Lomax), with Warrant Officers and Sergeants of the 1st Battalion at Sobraon Barracks, Colchester, on St David's Day 1951.

The 4th Battalion (TA) at the Festival of Britain Parade in Swansea on 2 June 1951.

A green and apprehensive National Serviceman, Private B. George, is kitted out at Maindy Barracks in December 1951.

Between 1951 and 1960 the Regimental Depot at Maindy Barracks, Cardiff, was heavily involved with the training of National Servicemen. Here, Dai Dower, the Welsh boxer, reports for National Service.

Korea-bound 2nd Lieutenant John Bowler bids farewell to his mother at Southampton Docks on 10 October 1951. Mr Bowler returned safely from the war and was awarded the Military Cross for gallantry.

1st Battalion National Servicemen in Korea on St David's Day 1952. These members of the HQ Company wear the traditional leek on their berets. Left to right: Pte L. Baker, Pte K. Davies, Pte B. Richards, Pte L. Campbell, L. Cpl J. Ford, Pte 'Win' Price.

The 1st Battalion in Korea on St David's Day 1952. Despite the wartime conditions, traditions and customs were, as far as possible, maintained. Private Leonard Smith, the youngest soldier in the Battalion, is seen here eating the leek accompanied by a roll on the drum.

The 1st Battalion in Korea, 1952. Left to right: Corporal L. Jones, Corporal W. Davies and Private E. Smith search reserve positions for North Korean infiltrators.

The 1st Battalion in Korea in April 1952. Major D.E.B. Salmon of The Welch Regiment takes over the Hill 355 position, Kowansan, from Captain J.C. Coles of the 45th United States Infantry.

The 4th Battalion (TA) Bren Gun carrier section in the Summer of 1953.

The street lining detachment of the 5th Battalion (TA) for Coronation Day. Left to right, back row: Pte R.H. Rees, Pte C. Lewis, Pte C. England, Pte M.D.L.I. Davies, Pte T.J. Hawkins, Pte W.F. Evans, Cpl G. Cowell, L. Cpl T.I. Jones. Middle row: L. Cpl K. Berry, Cpl P.W. Cotter, Cpl V.J .Bendall, Lt G.W. Woodyat, Sgt W. Richards, Cpl B.H. Morris, L. Cpl R. Rigby. Front row: Pte W.A. Edgeworth, Pte W. Griffiths, L. Cpl W.V. Jones, Pte G.G. Gibbs. They wear the then newly introduced No. 1 Dress with Dragon collar badges.

Civilian to Soldier – the transformation is completed with the Passing Out Parade of National Servicemen at Maindy Barracks, Cardiff, c. 1953.

The 4th Battalion (TA) at Regent's Park Zoo, 6 September 1953. 'Sospan', a new Goat Mascot, joins the Battalion.

Officers of the 1st Battalion in Hong Kong on October 1954. Only the front row can be named: left to right: Major D.E. Thornton, Major J.S. Martin, Major P.F. Skuse, Major B.E.W. McCall MC, Lt Colonel B.T.V. Cowey DSO, Major M.C.P. Stevenson MC, Major E.D. Lloyd Thomas, Major H.E. Byrde, Major R.N. Randell.

A Guard of Honour from the 1st Battalion, The Welch Regiment, on 6 August 1955. The occasion was the visit of Her Majesty, The Queen to Haverfordwest and Pembrokeshire.

K.J. Davey (team captain), holding the trophy, and 1st Battalion rugby team, winners of the Army Rugby Cup on 28 March 1956.

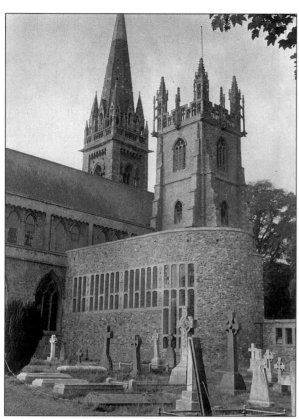

The Welch Regiment Memorial
Chapel, Llandaff Cathedral,
Cardiff. It was dedicated on
22 September 1956 by His Grace,
the Lord Archbishop of Wales.

The 1st Battalion British Army of the Rhine on manoeuvres near Luneberg, 1956.

Corporal Conway Jones of the 6th Battalion (TA) and the Battalion's Goat Mascot, 1957.

The caption on the photograph reads: 'Greek meets Greek'. The Pioneer Sergeant of the 1st Royal Welch Fusiliers meets the Pioneer Sergeant of the 1st Battalion, The Welch Regiment in Cyprus, 1958. The Pioneer Sergeants of the British Army are by tradition allowed to wear a beard.

Colonel J.E.T. Willes inspects the 1st Battalion Quarter Guard at Benghazi, Libya, in April 1959. This was the first guard to be armed ceremonially with the SLR (Self Loading Rifle).

Anti-Tank Platoon, 1st Battalion, Benghazi, Libya, 1959.

Her Majesty, Queen Elizabeth II, presenting new Colours to the 4th, 5th and 6th (TA) Battalions, The Welch Regiment, at Cardiff on 6 August 1960.

The 6th Battalion, The Welch Regiment (TA). The Battalion Goat Mascot meets schoolchildren at Ballater, Scotland, in July 1961.

'Dewi' – the new Goat Mascot – joins the 5th Battalion (TA) at Regent's Park Zoo in 1962. He, like other regimental Goat Mascots, was a descendant of the Royal Herd which once roamed Windsor Great Park.

The 1st Battalion Colour Party at the Queen's Birthday Parade at Berlin Sports Stadium, 1962.

Men of 'A' Company, 1st Battalion, on the East/West Berlin Border Patrol, Berlin Garrison, 1963. They wear steel helmets which display the white, red and green regimental flash. White metal Dragon collar badges and the shoulder flash 'The Welch Regiment', white on a red ground, can be seen.

The 1st Battalion, The Welch Regiment, acting as a demonstration battalion at School of Infantry at Warminster, 1963. The crew are demonstrating a General Purpose Machine Gun.

Captain John Ayres briefing a platoon of the 1st Battalion when on exercise in Jamaica in April 1965. Note that all ranks wear the gilding metal title 'WELCH' on their shoulder straps.

The 6th Battalion (TA). The Goat Major, Goat Mascot and Drum Major head the Battalion which is marching through Cardiff to entrain for annual camp, Summer 1965.

The 1st Battalion, October 1966. Lieutenant M.F. Adler (far right) and Sergeant 46 E. Harris (far left) are seen here with the Battalion's United Nations Platoon at Youngsan, Korea.

A Battalion Internal Security Platoon from the 1st Battalion at the Hong Kong Garrison, 1966-7.

A patrol from the 1st Battalion, Hong Kong Garrison, at work in the mainland New Territories, 1966-7.

The 1st Battalion, The Welch Regiment, on parade at Stanley Fort, Hong Kong, 1967.

The 1st Battalion, Stanley Fort, Hong Kong, 1967. The Colonel of the Regiment, Major General F.H. Brooke CB, CBE, DSO, meets Major P.L. Cutler (Second in Command) Captain and Adjutant P.T. Johnson and RSM 84 R.V. Williams.

Major General Frank Hastings Brooke CB, CBE, DSO, Colonel of The Welch Regiment, takes the salute at annual reunion Church Parade of Old Comrades, Llandaff Cathedral Green, Cardiff, 1968.

1st Battalion, Ghana, 1968. The Commanding Officer, Lt Colonel L.A.D. Harrod, introduces Regimental Sergeant Major Bert Pennington to a senior Ghanaian army officer.

A soldier of the 1st Battalion, The Welch Regiment, on exercise in Ghana, West Africa, September 1968. He wears the white, red and green battalion flash on his jungle green hat.

The 1st Battalion, The Welch Regiment, on parade at the Royal Hospital, Chelsea, to celebrate the 250th anniversary of the raising of the Regiment on 14 March 1969.

Men pose outside the main gate of the old Regimental Depot prior to the amalgamation ceremony of 11 June 1969. They are, left to right: an unidentified sentry, RSM Bert Pennington, Lt Colonel P.L. Cutler MBE, the 1st Battalion Goat Mascot and the Goat Major, Major General F. H. Brooke CB, CBE, DSO, Colonel of The Welch Regiment, -?-.

Amalgamation Day Parade at Cardiff Castle, 11 June 1969. This picture commemorates the event when the 1st Battalion, The Royal Regiment of Wales (24th/41st Foot) was formed. The amalgamation of the 1st Battalion, The South Wales Borderers, and the 1st Battalion, The Welch Regiment, was presided over by HRH The Prince of Wales who, as Colonel in Chief, presented the Colours to the new Regiment and also formally accepted, on their behalf, the Freedom of the City of Cardiff.